A BIRDSONG STEMS THE TIDE

By
Matthew Bottiglieri

Copyright © 2021 by A.B.Baird Publishing
All rights reserved. This book or any portion thereof may
not be reproduced or used in any manner whatsoever
without the express written permission of the publisher
except for the use of brief quotations in a book review.

Printed in the United States of America
First Printing, 2021
ISBN 978-1-949321-25-8

All writings within this book belong to the author.
Cover Design by: Max Estes
Illustrations by: Max Estes

A.B.Baird Publishing
66548 Highway 203
La Grande OR, 97850
USA
www.abbairdpublishing.com

For Jen -
Light of my light
Heart of my heart

TABLE OF CONTENTS

Introduction	P. 1-2
A Birdsong Stems The Tide	P. 4-5
She	P. 6
Not Me Forget	P. 7
Bitter Flower	P. 8
Renoir's Shadow	P. 9
Fertile Crescent	P. 10
Pilgrimage	P. 11
Forgive Me	P. 12
Ashes To Ashes	P. 13
Sing Sing	P. 14
Surrender	P. 15
Quietude	P. 16
Let's Let The Stars Unmake Us	P. 17
The Lizard	P. 18
Creation	P. 19
Magpie	P. 20
Permit Me	P. 21
Night	P. 22
Mourning	P. 23
Night Sonnet	P. 24
Malta	P. 25
Dagger	P. 26
Wield Me	P. 27
Hands	P. 28
Endura	P. 29
Solamente	P. 30
Pelear	P. 31

She Says	P. 32
Radiant Joy	P. 33
Lunch	P. 34
The Scorpion	P. 35
Ode	P. 36
E.F.	P. 37
Nihilists' Brunch	P. 38
Frozen Memoirs	P. 39
End	P. 40-41
Fever Dream	P. 42
Leonora Carrington	P. 43
Minotaur	P. 44
Moon-Bitten	P. 45
Jen	P. 46
Chet	P. 47
Ode To Renee Margritte	P. 48
Home	P. 49
Ode To Paul	P. 50
Again (Looking at Old Photos)	P. 51
The Red Angel	P. 52
Hymn To Saint Water	P. 53
Lark's Shriek	P. 54
Augury	P. 55
Yours Sincerely	P. 56
Ghost Coronation	P. 57
Ode To Dreaming Cities	P. 58
A Lover In Three	P. 59
Ode To Creation	P. 60
Mothersong 125th	P. 61
Manhattan	P. 62

Paris As Viewed By Brassai	P. 63
Loss	P. 64
What Is Left?	P. 65
Titania	P. 66
Picasso	P. 67
Hecate	P. 68
Maine	P. 69
Birds	P. 70
Song Of Absent Lovers	P. 71
Song Of My Father	P. 72
Adze	P. 73
let Me	P. 74
Mr. Mink	P. 75
Mr. Shadow	P. 76
Sonnet	P. 77
Apartment	P. 78
After Reading Lamantia	P. 79
Ode To Adonis	P. 80
Hill	P. 81
Communion	P. 82
A Whip To Teach	P. 83
Magia Negra	P. 84
Mother	P. 85
Heat	P. 86
Disembodied Dream	P. 87
Only He Can Sing	P. 88
Syntatic	P. 89
Madam Magpie	P. 90
Joyce	P. 91
Time	P. 92

Again	P. 93
Scorpion King	P. 94
The Eye	P. 95
Lisboa	P. 96
Sonnet Of Wind And Sun	P. 97
Eclipse	P. 98
Breaking	P. 99
Recount	P. 100
Drown	P. 101
Final Sonnet	P. 102
Photo	P. 103
Estrella De Noche	P. 104
Lorca's Sonnet	P. 105
Chemise	P. 106
Creation Song	P. 107

INTRODUCTION

It begins and ends with words. Words grafted upon images. Art informed by the pulp of terse sentences. Light blooming in the joy of an empty heart. Long days of truancy sharpening pencils into arrowheads and stringing bows with necklaces of blistered sunlight. The myth called me from a place of scales and feathers. Of horrifying reflections and maidens chained to damp stones. It echoed from Atlantean waves and lost dreams of gold, porphyry, and other occult joys. Books. Art. Profanity and a steady diet of comics. Superheroes, mostly. There were films, of course, and thousands of albums. Punk rock. Bad Brains. Northern California thrash metal. Miles Davis. Coltrane. Wes Montgomery sliding thumbs across molasses. A joy birthed from the agony of failure. The falling and the breaking. The lost boulevards and the acerbic voice of Burroughs. The junky saint. The mad shaman of the final chapter. Skinheads pounding the gates. The filth and the fury. Puerile dreams of arches and redhead babysitters. Nevermind the Bollocks. Blisters. Plains. Shields of saddened stars and trips to desolate cities. It's all in there. The compost and the dregs. The underachievement. Wrestling my way through my teenage years. The long runs through the dark. Churning my innards as I died for water to calm my blistered throat. There were the swords. The fist fights in the school hallways. The epileptic fugues. The boxing. There was, of course, skeletal Irving Feldman. The living ghost who encouraged me to lace my shoes and step on the mat. Of course, there's Creeley. Wodan. The father of terse, honest language. The voice I had no idea that I longed to hear. Susan Howe taught me to write honestly for the dead - those who can neither see nor hear. She taught me that a poem lives two lives. It buys real estate on the page. It also lives in our ears and hearts. It sings to us from its cenotaph. I didn't understand her work until I visited Boston's Granary Cemetery. Her poems became epitaphs. Scratched out grave rubbings. Palimpsests and imprecations. John Yau pried open the door and showed me the way forward. Surrealism. Images. Meanings-within-meanings. I loved his words so much that they threatened to become my words. I lovingly placed him aside so that I could find my own voice. I stopped speaking for twenty years, so that I could speak as cleanly as a bell. The journey continues. I visit John, from time to time. We speak as though we're old friends. We are, in a sense. It always comes back to the word, though. The primal talisman. It begins and ends with words. Vessels. Contagion. One image bleeding into another. An ugly beauty, to quote Monk. An ugly sadness that stirs me like the threads of a bow. Music. A voice breaking as it scrapes across Lethe. Old ghosts. Bones. Feathers. Paint. Words. Sounds.

A BIRDSONG STEMS THE TIDE

A birdsong stems the tide
The sky unpins its reveries
And dips her feet in my mouth
While I lay dreaming at the ankles of sleep
And feel a voice's crush-
Breasts carving me with their fervent diamonds
Suffocated by the thrust of sleep-
By the feathered lips of a blackbird's shadow
I am pinioned between waltzing flame
And the heat that refracts the air
The haze of the road that's woven
A textile of sighs to shroud me
Days measured in nautical miles
In knots to climb downward from this tower
From coins used as buttons
From the story we tell ourselves
Of iridescent birds roosting in ribs
In the song of our lives
And the hearses of burning axles
I see across a hill until I scrape
The belly of a haunted lake
Old longings' feverish lycanthropy
Silver to banish woodland demons
A sword slaying the ululating dragon
Squamous dreams to crawl across my skin
I remain vestal in the boiled vegetable marrow
In all the roads that reach the ancient town
To citadels that guard tenantless stars-
The past is conjugated by the present
My knees are broken at the joint of longing
Zodiac in the sting of my constellations
A joyous beast tears from my throat
Watch over me, chthonic lust

Bury your flower in my hip
Boil me in the darkness of your embrace

SHE

The curvature of a vase
Milk of porcelain
Left partially eaten
Fruit of the bitten flower
Raining behind the drawn
Shades of her gray eyes

A star to pin itself
To a wound festering in Heaven
Old flowers old flowers
Offered from the inimical angles
Three of them
Old damp roots
Calling in utter darkness

The leaves whisper their quiet flame
Watching the night lick the bones of
Elegant shoulders
Blades to slice the wind in half
Singing the song of fallen summers
Felling a tree inside our needful bodies

NOT ME FORGET

Now that the city sleeps and nights smolder, I am able to speak the language of this harrowing. I don't trust the shearing of these moments, nor do I have the will to chase you, fey specter of fragrant wind. Catullus had his Lesbia - the one who nearly broke him. I have nothing but this anguished emptiness. Love is a needful pocket - the ache of hunger snarling at the belly. I can taste the sound of bitterness. It breathes from my pores when I feel your diffident laugh carve me like a lathe. I need not mention that you're more worth that you're trouble, but the manner in which you present yourself to me like a basket of dark olives is enough for me to bite the floor with my knees and beg you to scrape my lips with your toes. I try to speak candidly with the lonely ghost of my heart but it's tantamount to arguing with a stone and you are a figment - so many women this bruised narrator has loved or longed to finish like half-eaten fruit - a body within which I'd nest and watch the day finish the remains of itself and feast on the breast of Mother Night. You, unnamed vestal of darkness, kiss my throat as I pry myself apart, as I scatter like riff raff or a flock of insouciant birds. Let me close you within my hands and cherish a frail moment. Let me close my eyes and drown the taste of your shadow. Permit me to remember so that I may forget.

BITTER FLOWER

You, body of broken pillars. You, hills of rotting fruit. Sea of torn, unripe paper. Is that wind brushing your hair with cold fingers? Who placed that kiss of blood on your face? Or that wingspan darkening your sensuous lip? What are the names of the cats gleaming in your joyful eyes? Who spilled the coffee of your smooth skin? Who pieced your body together with fingers of bone? They say that you read until you became the words interred in your heart- that violent sex of color. When you couldn't move and you dreamed away your pain to distant vistas. You are a terraced pyramid. A mournful ziggurat. The thousand-faced lover. You are bruised and beaten, but your art persists. Its fiery wings carry you above open graves and broken bones. I'd eat the bitter flower that blooms and blooms and blooms from your body. I'd pray your feet to nest in the well of my mouth. I'd gnaw the ibis throat and watch you birth a euphoria of a thousand pigments. The aura of creation and the alchemy of lust. A gift to Earth in a million heartbeats. A sky filled with a sea of breasts. The riverbed of a willing body.

RENOIR'S SHADOW

I often think of Renoir's thick-armed men
Staring at swan-necked women with parasol breasts
Their tactile paleness begging me to reach
Forward and kiss their beautiful throats

I watch them unspool dark Parisian hair
In their sad boudoirs and curl their fingers
Through what's left of mine

They lead me like a blind man to their petit
Beds to fall inside them like a warm bath
O how I taste the canvass of their navels
And the lilac blush of their elegant breasts
I'd sing them a pallet of vibrant thrusts
I'd break them in a fever of relentless brushstrokes

FERTILE CRESCENT

Tiamat to Akkad to the river that runs both ways, summoning the body of antediluvian lust. The immortal sleeps the death of sleep, and the king mourns the death of his compatriot - that breaker of bulls. Furious are the eyes of Marduk - watcher of the within and the without. The multi-faced bitch devours priests and smashes bones on the cheeks of the ziggurat - a Babel of birds with sharpened beaks - a flood of bodies that drowns the world - a man measuring his lust in cubits. This is the falchion covenant - a refracted necklace, a bent neck and willing body - sunlight of bovine breasts - a sky god dragging its wet tongue through a crescent. A sandstorm fucks the sky and births a Babylon - Sumer of the cuneiform serpent. The gods give us their disorder - their will to nourish the fields with blood. Gilgamesh tramples the throat of lands a demon following a trail of blood - he the underworld mourner, the butcher of beasts raging. The gods who keep their secrets, their profanities, and their primal sins, while man tends to the fields of his lusts as clouds weep from the skies. The body longs for bodies; the land longs for floods.

PILGRIMAGE

I possess endless dreams that reveal
My body exchanging prayers with yours
My lips migrating like pilgrims across the
Mangroves of your breasts
To bask in the shade of that taut navel
To push further to lap silt from the life-giving delta
To inhabit the grooves of your prophetic steps
To drink from the oasis flower and gasp at clean stars

I would unfold above you like a tent
And tongue the throat of your ululation
I fill a skin like water to murder your thirst
My mouth's obeisance flutters the moth
We are one body beneath the naked moon
A whirlwind of blood that murders the sun

FORGIVE ME

Guard this box of flame
Body of Stalking Jaguars
Stars dictate the positions of our bodies
They preside above the fires that we birth
Striking the flint of our needful hips
Forgive my infidelities, Pale Morning
My mouth couldn't ignore the moon's breasts
Or the sweetness of her instep

I am alone now in this house of ruins
My fevered shiver a cawing of dead birds
I reach for you with dreaming fingers,
Lips of Falling Rain
Let me drink from the river between your ribs
Forgive me the trespass of my treacherous flesh

ASHES TO ASHES

You never taught me much father I guess because you were making it up in step poor Phaedrus you were endlessly lost you sad coin counting fool you Bronx sonnet you short madman you beautiful sinning traitor hard to fathom the number of women who loved you when you were a mess they lined up outside your door and I listened to you rut while I a lonely wrestler with an eager body had no one to share my bed as one remorseless screw bled into another through my door one or two smiled at my body as we both attempted a pee at the same time but they never knocked or parted the curtains and invited me to crawl through them like windows my sinew was agonized and young and aching for connection with anyone the loneliness was so sharp I could've bled myself with it you and I both yearned to be buried alive in the women who shared our beds you died in the arms of your love and you are now ashes to ashes gone and I remember the way you climbed inside those needful bodies to hide from yourself I wanted to swim inside a woman's darkness and feel alive until I'd cease to exist in a flicker of sorrow and return to the cage of my bones now that I am your age I understand your sadness and what you were running from and I am sad too but there's nowhere to hide and death is a fast runner

SING SING

I dipped my hands in you
River of sighs and suppurating roses
I flowered like a lotus
And sought water in your damp shadow
I sang you a lament when the moon
Broke its jaw on those terrifying walls
I am imprisoned in my own body
My bones screaming sonnets of escape

Ciudad of my past
Abusive mistress of the setting sun
You wounded me with the blade of your whisper
When I was a fledgling heart
I still bleed nightmares of strangled birds
Locked inside this disconsolate abattoir

SURRENDER

And I dreamed that you spilled across me
A cloud of birds too thick
To separate wing from beak
I chisel the broad jungles of your face
My tongue dredging the dark Amazon of
Of your heart that wound that splits you
I seek the handholds of your breasts
Where colorful birds peck the day's eyelids

Your jaguar's shadow stalks me through
The ruins of this sacred bed
I cannot see you in the mist's pungent breath
But my heart feels you in its resonant bones
Take me softly you murderous shade
I've gifted you my surrender

QUIETUDE

I sing the song of your quietude
The solace of the dark mountain's sleep
I watch a slip fall from you like a cloud
And bathe your delicious feet
In low-hanging mist

My mouth gives birth to plaintive
Birds when your eyes
Set my bones

Bear my weight you nest of
Axe-breasted moans
You lick of broad-leafed jungle
Draw your heart like a bow
And bury your poison in my hip
Leave me to the feast on your shadowed places

LET'S LET THE STARS UNMAKE US

Let's let the stars unmake
Us as the sea thirsts for water
As you dream and I wear the garb
Of a moon that aches to lick
The shadows of your breasts
I am motion-
The hands of a ticking clock

The heat that wishes to melt us
There is nothing but
The slumber of silence
Here in this wounded tenement
This house of wayward strangers
I knead constellations as the sky
Attends to its bruises

I am a coarse language unspeakably
Wallowing in the Hades of starlight
Dawn cuts me like a knife
As I festoon you with orchids
As I drink the scent of pollen
And the nectar of rain

I'd have you choke me
I would have you crucify this bed
Set me adrift like a northern mariner
Make this bed a pyre
Sing me the hymn of my passage

THE LIZARD

A hatchet-faced lizard
Pricks the ingenue with its spinster eyes
A newspaper accordions between
The necks of gazelles drinking away
Savannah heat-
Dark buttons blooming in kisses of blood

A man dreams of diving into
Her dark rivers of skin
Seared by a discomfited lizard
The young lady's yawn
Drags across his chest and teases his leg
Her beauty kills him

They lock eyes inevitably
Drawn together like magnets
A current flowers between their bones
The young man curls about the lady like smoke
And possesses her table like a succulent ghost
The lizard scurries like a bygone age

CREATION

Fire of fire blunting stone suns and rain striking like a stone hammer or bony lightning conceiving a giant serpent strangling the world's navel shedding its shadow within the sex of dying gods moaning to an expanded universe and the darkness draped across the heavens' pale shoulders it doesn't matter thirsty gods of a discarded pantheon the fucks of cosmic lovers boomeranging through infinite space running when the sky furrows her brow or bulls charge beneath the surface running from the atlatl and biting shadows kneading the agonized love of clay strong bodies beneath the scorpion sting of blistered stars creation myths perpetually manifested a birth giving birth to itself time flowing into a wound in its side time meeting itself for the first time time dying and shedding time

MAGPIE

And you let me watch you comb
A stream of nightfall teasing your shoulders
As twin moons carve names in your face
Beautiful magpie I sing
The perfection of your
Untouched breasts

I would lick them like a silk breeze
And watch you spill like cherry blossoms
From the frame of your window
Above the wet tree reaching with arthritic fingers
And the stars sharpening their knives
Kiss me with the sex of your voice

Daughter of the lilting hills
Body of the anguished bed
I poise like an archer to seek you
Like an obedient mutt
I am yours to use as you devise
Allow me to give yourself to you

PERMIT ME

Dagger of blooming roses
Anguished hand of clenched sorrow
Arch of succulent footstep
Embracing this churlish bed
Your body's foolish hour
Broken against what can't be broken

Carve me with your slumber
With the waves of your breath
Let me inhabit that space between spaces
Or hide like an ardent letter in your tight pocket
Perhaps i'll linger like a ghost or lazy shadow
Where the floor moans beneath your feet

The hours expand and contract
Much like the rise and fall of your chest
Which dream flowers inside you
As the night beats its stars like a hammer
Hand me a terrifying secret with your mouth
Permit me to open and close you like a door

NIGHT

The night has yawned and stretched
And stars burn in the kiln of its heart
A woman gathers dreams like arrowheads
Stone fangs to pierce the ash of her body
Dirty-footed deity the wind's breath serenades
The braiding of your languid form
Your voice punishes the moon's beating heart
Make a beast of this sorrow

I hand you this deserted palm to fill with your hand
Mana of breasts bitten by stars
Watch me hew the backs of these mountains
I a wide-chested peasant with a face as
Broad as wooden shield am one who fights
I would curl about your ankles like a sated jaguar
I'd stalk the wild things and place them at your feet
Mother Gaia I am yours to knead like river clay

Mother of death I am your arrow
Your basket of stolen hearts
I am the spirits that gnaw your arches
I am the dark hair of water that flows upward
I am the sorrow that steals men's faces
And walks on four legs
I am the stars' hunter and the moon's killer
I am yours

MOURNING

I'd brush you apart as birds fly from the sky's mouth and eat the remains of the night's unfinished fruit. Sometimes, I dangle my feet in the dusky waters of this bedroom and read the words that your body forms while you sleep. Mostly, I gather you and permit your breathing to carve me like a river. Spill into me, dark torrent of butterflies. Fill me, joyous lake of shadow. Sky of umbra and silk, empty your urn across my stomach. Shroud me like a sensuous eclipse. Finish me as though it were my first time - the thousandth time. Place a nest of swallows in the grave of my ribs. Pull the fire from my mournful equinox by its roots. Devour me, furious body.

NIGHT SONNET

Fatigue lashes me with her silent whip
My bones sink in the grave of this bed
These eyes are heavy with dull aches
An indolent robin nests in my mouth
Iguana yawns crawl from my throat
I should read a handful of poems
Or maybe fondle the night's soporific hips
Why not profess my love to the moon's breasts

Somewhere a wolf or lynx creeps below a star's belly
As I spit the rinds of words and pray
I can feel fatigue's caresses in my marrow
Her feet teasing the lips of my dreams
One more line and I finish
One more line and I'm hers

MALTA

Buildings of bleached bone
Caressing spilled shadows
Suns brushing their flaming hair
Body draped in the stillness
Sweat heading to jewels surround
A beautiful keyhole

To unlock a supine body with
The turning of hips
The arms moving to the
Pulse of hours
To harmonious thrust
A counterpoint moan

Bones clack like shimmering beaks
Kissing the moss of parted lips
Savor the taste of roots
Mineral spirits haunt my tongue
Churning to sublime release
Bright feathers devour the sun

DAGGER

I sing of broken song in exile
Windward the sadness draws its sword
And flaming birds cling to the sorrow
Of my chest
Turn me counterclockwise, my heart
Beating to spite its beating

Spirits of my soured blood
Your wounds summon monsters
You murder the best part of yourselves
You desiccated sparrows you
You covetous bastards
You've frayed to arthritic knots

And I have grown tired
The battered tin of my ears renders
Me to gargoyle magic to strangle
The throats of sibling liars
I can abide the blood-let of patricide
I break the daggers of my knees

WIELD ME

I have watched your succulent shadow
break the bones of needful beds
The beaks of your breasts feasting
on my lonely ribs
A bloom of flame sears
the rumor of my hips
I write elegies with the haunt of your body
My remains are yours to sweep

I long to rebirth in the grave of your body
To crucify myself on your heavenward chin
Break me you vengeful seraph
You burning spirit
Sheath me like a sword
Wield me like a horrid weapon

HANDS

It's dangerous to let oneself feel. To peel layers of years until you're nothing but smoke or vapor. When you're younger again. When you ache for your life to unfurl. When you place one foot in front of the other and your susurrations form the rhythm of your footsteps. I have returned to that quiet place of desperation. That place of fallen snow and comforting silence. I can see you and I answering questions. I see us conjoined like interlaced fingers, or holding hands in the dark. I see you in a park - tall and sharp cooing at birds. We have coffee. Our conversation expands and contacts like our shadows. We temporarily exchange hearts. We place them in each other's palms & study them like rare stones. Maybe we watch the sun complete its inevitable course & we let it guide us like a lodestone or compass. Maybe we enjoy dinner in a softly-lit cafe. Maybe you lead me back to your hotel and we answer questions with questions. Maybe we spend the night or an hour interlocked like Hieroglyphs. We form our own alphabet. Our own parts of speech. Maybe then we separate. Having said all we need to say. We return to the lives that we've carved for ourselves. Maybe we cleanse our hearts of these memories. These words that we gather like pearls. Or, maybe we never forget. We exchange a small part of our hearts. To saver, to hold, to recall when we're bathed in silence. When our loved ones are asleep and we're alone with ourselves. Maybe we'll return to one another during a sequence of dreams. An anthology of vaguely-interlocking chapters. Maybe our story is already written. All I know is that I lack answers. That I am the victim of my own heart. This, I can say: If you're out there, somewhere in the dark, waiting, I will find you, and we will take turns speaking with our hands.

ENDURA

My Endura my flame that
Cleanses flame
My ash that tastes the wind's body
Come to me in Manichaean devouring
Of lucid shadows be mine Endura
You flame of beautiful arches
Daughter of Persepolis moans
I scatter your body like birds

Pierce me with the darts of your breasts
Abide the tongue that cleanses your feet
Sound the ache of my thieving bones
Give me the desolation of your hips
The wraith of your submission
Grasp my body like a sword

SOLAMENTE

After this, I'll be the blade that wounds itself
The empty-handed mouth starved of words or speech
I've said all that I can say
Now that I've watched you turn yourself like pages
And mouth the words I've fed you
I've witnessed you twitch like the tail of a cat
Saying things that ground to dust the bones of my heart

I'm despondent and listening to the song of the wind
An acidic ache rots the fruit of my heart
Tomorrow, I may sleep in the dark oceans of your eyes
Maybe I'll hoard these pains like a spinster and laugh
Today, I carve myself and wait
For the wind to scatter the pieces

PELEAR

See how she drives, sweet Pelear
As the ghost discards its umbrella
And flees the pagoda
See how she grasps the moon
By its blade and submits it
To her blinded will

See how the rain hides its
Secret lightning
Falling filthy as a hag's mane
See how the woman who fights
Slaughters a nest of cancerous serpents
She of drawn steel biting the gleam

She flanked by midnight priests
Of starless supplication
Gift her the piloting covenant
She in her damp untied shoes
Slayer of selfish ghosts
One half flame one half shadow

SHE SAYS

Baring her body like a dagger
Pain of drawn breath
In plumes of horny winters
New Years to fallen bones
And disharmony in rotting
Blackbird song of snow's death

Gathered in her arms
Thieves devour a boy
And makes him lap the milk of her skin
She crosses him like a pair of legs
Punctuating the sentences of his body
Don't be afraid she says

Draw me into you like breath, she says
Let me breastfeed your blood
Hollow me with that melody of a thousand wings
Carve your fears in the shrine of my bones
Float inside me, she says
She says

RADIANT JOY

I dream of Chagall's lovers
Their soft bodies dragged like kites
The woman revealing breasts of cloud
When her man removes her blouse
She probably shifts color as he
Plants himself inside her
His body flowering with pleasure
As her eyes draw like shades

Perhaps he steals behind and buries
Himself in her like a dagger
And she dies those sublime deaths
As flaming moths unspool
From her satisfied body
And bite a blue sky with their radiant joy

LUNCH

I'd go to lunch with you, maybe
And discover that my teeth
Are made of feathers when
I attempt to sink them into a warm baguette
(Something along those lines)
And a post lands in my lap
Obscurantism for its own sake-
Dreaming in strange colors
A sort of laughter that defies language
The great middle finger to the trenches
A world from which I am far removed
Too distant to smell the death of 1916

You can read the news in many ways
A slice through the center
A sword stroke as keen as laughter
A joy that transcends time and place
Utter senselessness making sense-
Despite the context
Given what we're up against-
How the air expands our bodies
Until we are glorious, bloodshot
Balloons overlooking the tarnished streets
I'll remember this conversation
This handshake through milky pages

Dear forbearer, hand me this invisible torch
This *de novo* that belongs to neither of us-
(Perhaps to Aristophanes or The Satyricon)
Or the precincts of absurdity
Such is life, Tristan: the world doesn't care
It lives because it has to

THE SCORPION

The bones ache with disembodied longings-
A light screaming through the dark
Towards carapace of seas to churn
The breasts of lonely hillocks
To sting an eidolon drowning in water-
An acidic rapier drawn in poisoned thrusts

Dreaming winds time's backwards moans-
Blood boiled through wires
A banquet of lines attended by crows
By a noise of thirsting suns
Water given to water-
To the mouth that longs for its throat

O zodiac of burning hands-
Eyes to sever eyes
Keys to unlock furious navels
A noise lashed to strokes of sorrow
Water given to water's shadow
A venomous slash through orgasms of rain

ODE

Ode to the wind and the succulent rain. Ode to the simmering of your beautiful bones. Ode to your radiant flesh and the moans that break my back. Ode to the lash of your body and the doorway nested between your legs. Ode to the sea and the taste of salt. Ode to the thousandth dream clenched by the night's burning mouth. Ode to the time we carve with our joy and the stars that cry their choruses to the boiling dark. Ode to the pyre and the pain that blooms from our marrow. Ode to the tragedy of human relationships. Ode to the sorrow of leaving and the fading of memory. Ode to the names that steal their treasure from our memory. Ode to the song of your sleep, of the nest I build in your hair. Ode to the taste of your feet and bitter Pythagorean fruit. Ode to the angles and the melody that haunts the wind. Ode to the damnation of your body. Ode to the names I cry to the dark.

E. F.

You may be sticks and straw, now, or close to it. Waiting for hearse or soil. To Sheol and eternal silence. Sephardic in your sardonic laughter-your skeletal gums straining against the wax of your face. Your chapters empty their dust; piles of pared fingernails-a feast for moths. My verse exemplifies what one shouldn't attempt. A cautionary tale of images buckling under their weight. I often skipped your court to write poems about the manner in which a lover bit her lip when I slipped my hands inside her. When she fed me her blooming darkness. You used to laugh and laugh at my boorishness. My lack of sophistication. My anger. I was empty, then, and yearned to face the world beneath someone else's skin. I am here, now, and you will soon return to Adam. To primordial sin. To apples and lisping serpents. To the shroud of your sallow verse. Your musty life and stale letters. Your bitter tongue and acidic sadness. Take your deaf child and stuff her ears with unleavened pages. Who will mourn you? The stones and the naked trees? They may mourn you; no one will hear them.

NIHILISTS' BRUNCH

Let's compare notes, my friend
Notes and maps punctuated by a death's head
By the newsreel and the meticulous ledgers
By hard water and terrifying electrons

Our foreign tongues are identical
Gulag or the ovens (choose carefully)
The hard day's labor or the gleaming scalpel
The Reichstag or the Decembrists' purge
The Czar is now a hole filled with butterflies, *mon ami*
Play "Kristallnacht and Long Knife"
On the ribs of the frozen dead

How does one measure evil?
By sheer numbers?
Never mind the gypsies or the kulaks
Or the vampiric census
Never-mind the bollocks or the ghettos
Or the Armenian mounds
Here's to you, Mr. Murder

Communist...fascist...123
God is dead or murdered
Or maybe death is God
Perhaps God is godless
O, my sweet Stalin
My love, Hitler
I hand you both a bouquet of murder
A garland of slaughter
Ashes to asses

FROZEN MEMOIRS

A man carves his ear with a knife
And watches the sky part
Like the lips of a door

Snow inside her heart-
A seashore
Her body spread towards water
A cold kiss of mouth

Autumn cuts our bodies in half
As we watch a man spar with
The voice of the old radio

The moon dusts its irreplaceable hip
As the sky folds the remains of
Its warm laundry

Raining inside the empty cup
Of the spinster's heart-
An asphalt heart seasoned with ice

It snows because it needs to-
Old ghosts placating the living

END

I often laugh at my own laughter
The way it sounds similar to crying
Ironic that I often cry when something's funny
And I laugh at my own sadness
Especially when I move my jaw
Bickering with ghosts

I often lose the nerve to publish words
So much verse buried in shallow graves

Days slide by and I am older
Balder, gray, and leaning into ugliness
Which is both sad and happy

Silly, really, or unimportant
Which, I guess is humorous
Or something along those lines

Someday, I will inhabit a row as tightly
Arranged as a line of verse
I will nestle as compactly as syntax
My meaning, like my body, aligned to stone and soil-
To leaves and the shapes of passing birds

The will continue to disregard my being
Or the words that I never got around to speaking

I will return to the place in which I'll
Have no recollection of returning-
To the darkness that precedes birth

The Tao of soil and oblivion-
Time flowing in two directions
A river with neither beginning nor end

FEVER DREAM

A butterfly of lips - a pale death's head
Succulent as blood
A copse of fragile birds
A body found dreaming catlike chases

A cat o'nine tails licking acidic laughter
A nervous flowering
A folding of walls
Saliva ringing a beautiful navel

Chewed moth wings powdering a
A lean cat's whiskers
A tongue slowly ragging a wound
A hiss of schools flying in keening slashes
Light calling for its shadow

LEONORA CARRINGTON

Time leaps from a claw-handle faucet
She, being Leonora, renders herself
In dryads of subdued patches
A running of horses

A kite flies a kite across of floor of tidy squares
The blue chair - coffin plush
Sings a dreamy aria to crucified wood
A sort of scream drowning in lush pigment

Sweet Leonora ignored, despite
The shapes singing through her hair
A thatch of naiad breasts to tease
Yolk-colored stars-
A mangled hand to calm the hyena rampant

Sweet face of wax buttons
Crows caw from your polished feet
From the riding crop of your spine

Smile through the spilled milk of your complexion
Betray the lover inside your lonely secrets
Dream the world beyond the your world of sleep

MINOTAUR

Furtive as thieves, we circle
Bitter with flowering acid
With a thousand years
Sprouting from our feet-
A hymn of a dead bird's cawing

The sky's bruise darkens
As we feel the bones' laughter
In the eye of your leavened sinew
In the abyss of our joyous hearts

Man of my blood
We kick and scream
Inside the pulp of this earthbound womb
We grind our teeth and clack our horns
Locked in sorrowful embrace

MOON-BITTEN

A blade of moon-bitten light cuts across
The fabric of my bleeding places
Estrella, I spill this basket of songs
Commemorating the dark seas
That swim the fathoms of your haunted lips

Drown me in their worrisome depths
As stars suture your hair
As I hold you safely in my blistered palm
O, my beautiful flaming shadow
My terrifying Kali of the bitter mouth

Split me down the center with your tongue
Watch a million manumit in specters
Of scintillating, abalone light
Slash me, you sweet dreaming sword!

JEN

Your body sings through the fields of my bones
If effaces the monuments of my prideful missteps
It places a soothing hand to quiet starless seas

Remember the flight of my joy
My sweet cotillion flower
Light of my light; heart of my heart
Heart that beats against mine

We lock in the flight as seasons turn their soil
We return to one another - wholly one
Wholly separate

CHET

To speak soft plumes of blue nectar
Lullaby Chet of brass
Lost in the silvered haze of sighing

Tarnished coins - the face one day
Hard as polished wood

A skeleton with a dying angel's throat
Embouchure's slow filing of melancholic waves

To lounge on a rotten beach in death's shadow
A whip of sand from the knave of a lover's curves

Lean towards me, sweet shadow

ODE TO RENEE MAGRITTE

Once the days cast off the last of their heat
The moon opens its tidy door
The crow dons a damp shawl
And squawks "checkmate" to a burning shrub-
A lonely figment of waste and pulverized stone

Renee sees death in the slate-colored breast-
The rising of knees of the slumbering goddess
Birthing flaming keys that she places in the
Artist's ugly, arthritic hand

Between fingers that witness the violence
Of fevered brushstrokes - similar
To wounding falling rain with a stiletto

So much for the man in the chapeau-
Or the hawk heavy beneath the mourner's coat
So much for the day's outmoded fashion-
Its tedious envelopes of junk

The only constant is the sex of coy seasons
The prophecies or oracular Mr. Crow-
Contentedly watching his ziggurat burn

HOME

I call you home, my warm flower
You, the laughing glow that soothes
The agony of my ribs

I hold sleep in your hands-
As your calm breath creaks the bones
Of this warm bed

You are the warm light that leads me
Through the cold cold night
A simple embrace offering solace
In the drawn bath of your hair

Returning until I cannot return
I see you in the warm splotches
Of love in unadulterated hues

The joy that radiates from your
Face's soft angles-
The smile that comforts me to sleep

I return until I cannot return home
I surrender to this warm verse

My lips pressing the flower of your lips-
Safety within the beats of your heart

ODE TO PAUL

My love was places I'd dreamed of inhabiting
Of wading the river of a lover's sleep
Paris sliding like a crimson slip
From a dark shoulder

I clasp the gold hoop between my
Aching teeth-
As I moan like a floorboard
When she presses me with the weight
Of her beautiful feet

The pigeons dream Cyclopean dreams
Of underwater places-
A backwards-swimming nymph
With squamous arms
And the brine of wet lips

The sun dances gray above
The molten slate
A color or fevered ships drifting
To foreign ports

Old Paris near the bank-
Sound or knives striking cobbles
A worn book tucked at right angles
Laughter sprouting wings in the dark
A song making love to shadows

AGAIN (Looking at Old Photos)

I see Paris caress your
Face with thickening shadows
As I mouth the ache of
Your body - a prayer
That bleeds its way to Heaven
And leaves an ache in my bones
I dream of tasting the textile of your
Immaculate flesh
I'd roll you across the landscape of my tongue
To swallow the flames of your
Beautiful feathers- that part of you that tears
My heart from its cover and scatters its pages
My mouth longs to write its filth across you-
Or carve the grottoes of your center-
That soft line that longs for shade
Please, sharpen yourself and split me in half
Let me bury my hatchet in your arches
Or shriek across your profligate seasons
Kill me with the dagger of your little deaths
Again and again

THE RED ANGEL

Blue Methuselah wears his burning pages-
As the red seraph closes one eye
And sorrow's hair flows upward
To lick blood from her navel
The night devours the griffin's smile
As she serenades the Azure Christ-
His stick-figured Golgotha a theater
Of broken legs and weeping
Light a candle to illuminate the friction of their flesh
Her orgasms closing like shutters
To shudder the night's bruises
A tongue drags across the moon's filthy arches
The old man clutches his Talmud-
A skein of Hebrew sharp as flames
Mary Magdalene bares her sad breast-
Dreaming away her winter-
A sighing of primary color

HYMN TO SAINT WATER

Saint Water wading through
Inverted trees toward the sacred
Heart a profane bird - engorged
With flames and missing a shadow
Musing on the nature of moss
And scalloped laughter

Saint Water returns to the Eucharist
Of his birth - a wife of berth
The Whore of Babylon singing
Through the gap in her front teeth
Ode to St. Water as joyous
The ghost or crust of custard

The way is paved with pages
And warm bread cooling
The leavened joy radiating
The belly of laughter's belly
Take my hand, Prince Pimpernel
Let us undertake this silly pilgrimage

LARK'S SHRIEK

Lark's shriek of breasts
Time moving across its stillness
Ocean grinding its teeth
The song tying its own knots

Restless dream's requiem
House of swollen vespers
The ululating thrumming
Seasons of drawn bowstrings

AUGURY

For the liminal ghost
Sacred stone altar
Perhaps a divinatory haven
Crows of long fingers furrowing
The steaming twists of dawn
Spearing with two heads
The eyes feast upon cats
Living in pairs

Ashes twist through the dark
Red fairy lights go sing their deaths
The tongue speaks of shapes
And chthonic visages - feral and unclean
The well in her soles a cauldron
From which the specter rears
The archon of augury
Hieroglyphic Hierophants burning
Their robes in hells of speech

Oracular the tongue speaks its feathers
To wound the trysts of crepuscular stars
Constellations mouthing the hymn of creation
Forked goes the Midgard slitherer-
Wolf shadow to norn

YOURS SINCERELY

I swim the lake of your body
While long-necked birds slash
The sky with the swords of their beaks
The day blushes as the sun overturns
Its chipped saucer - as I tongue your heart
Soft shuriken of my lips, slay
Me with your fulsome midnight
Murder me with the morning's poison

I find you in predatory bones of soil
And the thick chiming of iron bells
Plant me a garden so that my
Gazebo may perch and French kiss
The remains of the wind's ceaseless chatter
Infect me with the bee sting of your breasts
My sweet hummingbird-
My deathly sorceress

I write you this letter in agonized
Hurricanes of dark ink
And the lazy script of half-eaten sentences
Glorious feathers of light, quit asking
Me to lick the bottoms of your shoes
Stop casting darts at my wounds
And let me remember the perambulation
Of your tangled laughter

GHOST CORONATION

The screaming cages long
To confine their etiolated birds
Birds that have emptied their
Wings of gray dust and taken
To fingers of branches -
Desperate trees longing for
The magic of touch
The communion of still water

Seas of manic faces shift
Across the abscessed crags-
Ghostly coronations - smoke thin
Faces twisting in feudal depths
Fealty to kingdoms of marrow
And gristle hardened on the end of pikes
Galleries of rusted swords
Pollute the burial mounds

Times of famine feast on filthy tables
Filled with truculent potentates
Who dream syphilitic as they grind
Their yellow teeth
Caressing time's marbled fat
The day crams tallow in its rotting larder
Lauding the ovulation of the sky's stomach
Plotting their courses - profaning

ODE TO DREAMING CITIES

Feasts for the hungry mouth
The ovulating light of the gibbous breasts
Swirls for stars to break
The sleeping body of the city-
Taut ropes of cobbled streets
Arrant bedroom light
Colloquies of knaves
Gathering like pigeons
Life and life and life growing
From rich soil
From the drawn blade of laughter
And darkness overturned

A LOVER IN THREE

O to those few simple lines
The feast of curves that utter
The silence of parted lips
Birds flying in soft circles
While the rain mourns the
Sun's disquiet and
She a distaff unpins
The wilderness within
The flight of her heart

ODE TO CREATION

Jazz elocution in the jaundiced morning
The throaty language of birds in the
Beastliness of the burning oxcart
Geometry of gestures marinating
The seasons of eternal blushes
The secret orchard in slashes and
Quiet blossoming of cherries
A pilgrim's progress through the
Quotidian hades of smoldering love
That sex demoniac that splays red wings

Turnings of soil seasoning the blood
Of alchemies radiating from
Pale sorcerous hands-
The gnostic hymn sung in reverse
The history and orgasmic salons
The acrid lash of whips harvested
In a scream of calloused pigments
Art for the sake of the dead
For the souls lost in the tenebrous scrum
Art for the sake of art!

MOTHERSONG 125TH

Walk the skin of invisible faces
The muzzle drawing the scent of beating suns
Hammering the gong pubis of the vermillion bird
Fires of bone trapped in death's throat

Jungian bitten to cores of mythic fruit

Strange beasts carve the bottomless sea
And attend séances to commune with the living
Revenants of thirsting stars threading
Dreams through the lobes of horizons' ears

There isn't any know
There is only the shifter who treads shadows
The great feathery shaman stamping the ash
Reading the rinds of the day's gasp

A hidden river bites the squamous tail
A tall tale teller speaking circumferences
A pyre of fierce verse bloody in gums
Stench of song rooted in sky

MANHATTAN

Blushing mermaids unspool their alkaline hair-
Ink squinting from boatswain's shoulder blade
Schooners groans their
Way to ports once teeming with Italians
Now a pile of rusted crates
The immigrants have moved
To quieter places and left the old ghettos to birds-
To the sepia of memory
And the echo of unheard laughter
These bridges commemorate
The spines of mythic beasts
Cathedrals of rusted shadows and forgotten prayers
A haven of a self-hating Orphic and a suicidal prophet
A Coptic stew of old bones and Bowery pine
The hypodermic towers lean close to
Overhear secrets gathered by wind
And light erupts like fisticuffs
The cabbies trace oily circles as
Secretive men cover their hearts in old newsprint
A man looks to intercede and rescue
An accosted woman-
But the scrum drowns his outstretched hand
The day spins like a filthy turnstile
The moon slides by -pale as the belly of a fish

PARIS AS VIEWED BY BRASSAI

She isn't what she used to be-
Paris dreaming in cracks of water
Her cathedrals glower in a haze
Of moth-eaten light
Sweet dreams, he tells her
As he weaves his hand through
Her soaked hair
He longs to darn her
Black eyes with the needle
Of his body
Or swim through her warm skin
As braids of steam lick
The bothersome night
How does one make love to
A beautiful city?
Or feel her orgasms sprout
Wings beneath one's feet?
How does this feast of shivering
Bodies track the fever
Of passing hours
How does one make love
To a city's dark heart?

LOSS
for Robert Creeley

Let us break the bread of
These monument sorrows
These combs of bone and
Slick scales too rotten to taste
Let us floss the day from our
Cheeks and the rust of coins
Knead mountains until they
Sigh immaculate deaths to stars
Look to the sharp-breasted moon-
A brass bell to chime against tongues

The day matters naught to
Us in the unleavened sea of your navel
Time hands us a bouquet of daggers
Time to stab the hours until they cease breathing

WHAT IS LEFT?

I, too, am touched by the marvelous
That lives in books that lean
Like tired gulls and speak their vigils
Their Orphic sorrows slashing the silence
With the blades of their words
Try writing your song through the keyhole
Of a lonely eye - through the mouth of
Of a bruised heart - a half-eaten pear
That shrieks in a cage of ribs
Come to me, curvature of words
Scrape your lips against my wounds
And tell me the virgin secrets of my birth
Drip me until sorceries sigh
Until I stand-subverted and inverted
And face my hideous face -
So so ugly, I compensate with the words
Of my blood and the agony of being
For the longing to say a true goodbye to
Ghosts and the love of watching the dark
Unspool her sensuous hair and bury me
Inside my body - inside this vortex of words
What is left to say? What is left? Silence

TITANIA

I am the bird that settles on the blushing sword
That sows seeds in the ash of a heart
Tumble with me in the scrum of leaves
In the caterwaul of our marrow
To arrive inside you late for the autumnal feast
Titania, I see you naked as a November tree-
A patch of fire glowering in the grotto of your hips
My knees bite like spears as my bones acquiesce
As I am burned in the scream of passing seasons
Watch me bleed in phases to gather you like coins
In my hands and foment new religions from your body
I will ascend you like a hill to commemorate in Druidic
I shall reach to complete this covenant in ashes
Dreaming through the night's sorrow
Devouring the cinders of what's left

PICASSO

Picasso strained to bridle you,
Queen of melting candles
You peer into the ice of a
Warped mirror to chew the metal
Of your origami ribs-
Your damp yawn folded in half

Hand me a tray of pickled doves
As you hold the day by the gums
And tease the blue sleeper with
Your bored, indolent foot
See how he twitches through dreams
Asphyxiated and flat as book a cover

The vase is little more than a swirl-
A suggestion in three dimensions
Your silence begs us to hear you
To watch you unfold and soften the
Creases of your bleached belly
To offer us the olives of your small breasts

As you trace doors in ghostly temples
Sweet prisoner, your orisons are thin
As sallow paper
Give me your pulpy hand
I will guide you from this bleak chamber
Hand me the menagerie of your heart-
Breathe

HECATE

Hecate, I swim through your
Tarnished length of bone
And tongue the stanzas of
Your starless flesh
Wolves tread across my remains
As you gather whispers and
Inter them in a sleepwalker's grave

You are a sacred number-
My doomed hieroglyph
My slumbering wishbone
And lake of butterflies
I sleep you to the crossroads
Of our threshing
To the damnation of our waking

Time hammers the pulse of time
An anemic fusion through doleful heat
Let us make haste and repair our broken selves
As we carve new bodies
From the clay of quotidian fevers
Descend upon me, frowning night
Pin me to the corpse of this elision
Become me, entirely

MAINE

Lightning drawn from its barometric sheath
Fraying a humid silence of swaying grass
Gentle murmur of waves threshing the
Slate-cold bay-
A thousand fireflies punctuate the
Dusk's elegantly outstretched hand

Rain gathers and longs to gossip
Longs to run its gentle hands
Across the Earth's willing body
Wants to commune with root
And stone as it licks the
Point of an elderly roof

Time grows old here among
The young lovers steaming their cars
Long shadows close to fires
Dancing like djinni with beautiful feet
A chiaroscuro bitten by light
A floral dress slipping from a shoulder

BIRDS

Carved your name in a tree while my eyes were closed
When I was barely awake and morning leaned towards me
As though I were light- as though it saw me as water
Days are composed of oiled components-
The parts often less than their sum
These days I am more stitched than sewn-
More cluttered than clean,
Wishing you were here to disassemble me and
Find the flaws within this faulty engine
You never taught me the samsara of engines
But you did speak to me through
A child's ornithology-one I colored myself
While snow fell upward and ants spoke in acrid scents
Which brightly colored bird did you become
When your engine seized?
I'd part that book and shift its pages like leaves
Looking for the Tao of adulthood, the color of a feather,
Or the analects of acceptance

SONG OF ABSENT LOVERS

Lodged in me like an axe
The day summons its
Fervent demons and
Dips its hands in the
Remains of the moon's
Fevered breasts

I brush apart her body
Like the lick of stained curtains
To suck the marrow from
The hum of a dream
From the shudder of a coffin
Of filthy birds

I speak her body without
Speaking her body
I make fervent use of my hands
With the listless soul of mouths
With the bitter root of my tongue
With the heat of my voice

I bury the wedge of my heart
In the soil of her body
I rise and am made whole again

SONG OF MY FATHER

A crow flies backward into the night's empty sheath
A dark place of feathered flames and absence
Sharp as a widow's shriek- Sheol's tattered hem
The past is written naked in a solemn room
It circles itself -a hungry cat fit to chase
Time longing for the watchmaker
Who attends to the celestial clock

The dawn breaks open the lid of its casket-
Dust gathering dust
A sweep of starless hair and smooth
hands to soothe the bitter taste
Death yearning to commune with its spectral hand
I nakedly sewing verse to my ugly skin
buttons to hold back this importunate tide
seeking the dust in my father

These predatory birds long to tear me
to chain me to the pillar of my bones
The sorrow lives within the cracks
in the empty spaces and the jaundiced
Tenements between breaths
I sing a song to my father

A song of the wind-scraped heath and desolate moor
I sing to the sacred spaces wherein
leaves burn in beautiful hues
And my heart frees a million birds
I sing for myself
I sing myself

ADZE

Adze of my heart, chop me in two pieces
Let me slip through the door of your navel
Light the lantern of my bones
Million-faced moth, let me lick your heart
Clean of its secrets
Use the burning whip of my tongue to wound the stars
You crude instrument, thresh my body's wheat
Open your ribs, praying hands
Harbor my secrets while you crest and break
You lonely voice, splintered
Accept me, my beautiful apogee
Accept me!

LET ME

Let me formulate you like a sentence, you beautiful archangel light. Loose upon me the salvation of the empty temple of your hips. Drive downward until I change my name and the road kicks dust in my mouth, and I choke to holler the blessing that clings to the roof of my mouth. Tell me the story of your lip - the myth of breasts shadowed by the outstretched wings of the horizon. Come to me now, you succulent cannibal and lay with me in cenobitic night. Set upon me like a sun and scatter me like warm ash to burn the bottoms of your feet. Be Kali of the hellish skin for me. Trounce my bones. Devour my soul as I tongue your navel - a key to part your legs. I will roost and watch you sleep. I will vanish inside you and fold about you, sweet silence.

MR. MINK

Hustle Mr. Mink over a thrush's bones
To the fisherman's tackle

Hungrily, you move-
A finger of darkness scratching
Across a boat deck for snarls of bait

I stand at the harbor, younger and lighter
Watching a furtive weasel
Steal someone else's labor

I can see old men hauling the day's catch
And that bastard mink biding its miserable time

Hidden in some chink of wall or down
From the wooded hills

Indifferent to me as the currents of this quiet fjord

I feel insignificant and far lazier than that pesky mink

MR. SHADOW

The sun winds its watch
As wind howls through the spaces
In the mountain's teeth
And clouds arranged like tombstones
Deface their plush epitaphs and
Vanish like fragments of overheard gossip

Most of my friends were born
During a dragon's year
I was born rabbit - a decidedly urbane creature
Who's courteous to a fault

My ears twitch when the clouds reveal their empty graves
And wind scrapes bony mountains

My nose twitches when the scythe hisses
And lean Mr. Shadow introduces himself-
When death strolls towards me, backwards

SONNET

Sonnet of the blooming ache
Sonnet of the lonely bedroom
Sonnet that doesn't know
Sonnet of moans between lips
Sonnet of axe and stone
Sonnet of whimpering she
Sonnet of mournful nothing
Sonnet of flowering blood

Sonnet of her secret body
Sonnet of merciless laughter
Sonnet of the moon's ego
Sonnet of the sun's climax
Sonnet of wind and rain
Sonnet of sonnets

APARTMENT

What is don't want you to stop? she says
As moonlight breaks across her skin
As I rake her hair with my agonized fingers

We are both villains beneath judgmental stars
The stone beneath our bodies cold as brittle air

My mouth would meanly feast upon her body
As she peeled her skin offered a riddle
For my tongue to solve

That lonely apartment was haunted by filthy ghosts
She dissolved inside me and I forgot my sorrow
The loss of self that accompanies the whittling of days

We were joined in our loneliness, threshing and biting
The frayed tangles of our bodies-

Breaking each other in all the right places

AFTER READING LAMANTIA

My flightless bird, naked in your heart
Of sculpted daggers
Rip pages from my body and burn them
In the ash pits of your eyes

Sing me the lullaby of pale windows
Bury the knife of your lips in the gloom of my lonely hips
Flower from my mouth, you elegant prayer
Repeat me again a thousand times

Let wash myself in the cup of your hands
Let us make pretty use of our time
As the night screams
And stars hunger for our bones

I am yours, sweet sonnet to fill you like water
Feed me the story of your immaculate breasts

ODE TO ADONIS

Fire lives within its heat
I write verse with the lick
Of a blistered feather
With a tail of light to guide
Me through the starless dark

The night has a voice
And throat filled with tears
It screams its unknowing
Into a silence and shatters
The glass of this sacred house
This temple of swaying grass

Sing me poems from the crystal
Of your smoldering neck
Unyoke your cart of scintillating
Doves and bite the skin of my hand
You dreaming shadow and inert
Mangrove of broken whispers

Ululate through my bones
Hidden prince of shy houses
I too mourn the death of fathers
Tucked inside the shadow of
A psychopomp's span
Plant a seed in my heart
Guide the lisp of my hand
Catch me while I fall to Earth

HILL

Prayers to the thrush's neck
And the scimitar of flaming gold
Dragon's throat of piping flame
Heat slithering to seek water
Heat to pound metal into skin
Calls to the brass mercy of suns
Blades drawing its shadow and
Flowers of blood in the pirate's house
Crimson path to the last lonely hill-
That church of flayed ghosts

Brian, sweet Brian, I harvest your smile
And wear it around the circumference of my throat
Your leopard growls tear my crying heart
The choir of your hands breaking me whole

COMMUNION

The breast of a door opens
To the gaping yaw of mountains
The pitch of this tired house
Lonely fog caresses the moors
Dreams communing in dreams
Prayers to the dying of the sun
Winnowed by autumn's scythe
Of summer - premature winter
Giving birth to naked copses of trees
Copulations in reverse

The city has no memory
Nor does it bear malice towards
Its congested streets
All that remains is the light shed by our bodies

A WHIP TO TEACH

Now is the thrum of the pulse
Blooming the heat of our bodies
Darning like roots to stab the Earth's belly
I, broken shovel, long to taste the honey
Of your dark breasts

The sigh that eclipses the lake of my thieving bones
Longing to starve you of your secrets
I'd burn the moth of your mouth
With my genuflecting tongue
A whip to teach your moans to walk backwards
Can you hear me, jealous moon?
I seek the fragrant pleasure of the dark
Of your coral flower
I wish to harvest your heat and
Treasure the light of your hips

Give me the splendor of your weeping flower
So that I may plant it in the socket
Of my body and water it with the bitten bridle
With the nectar of rushing blood

Let me burn this galley of raiding gulls
Watch their wings fan their own flames
Watch me gather the sweat that beads
Your dreaming navel
Let me lay in the bed of your prayers
Let me sheath you, sweet dagger

MAGIA NEGRA

Ahora, sink your teeth
In the clay of my bones
When the sun leaps
Like a red fever
When the seasons
Sharpen their blades

Perch upon the prow
Of my antique bed
Let me drag my hand
Across the scrimshaw of
Your pale breasts
Release your heart in auguries

Dying is upon us-
The murder of night feast
Of the will of our sinew
The needs of our ribs
Darn me with the mariposa of your hands
Lure me with the deep song of your heart

MOTHER

Time stands still now
In the cold's unkempt hair
And the sighing of this
Voluminous house
You await the noise of geese
And the wild cats that
Carry their young in clean mouths

The day is weighed down by
The past's pile of junk
The old wounds that haunt our
Aging skin and the planks of our bones
To speak candidly with you into that
Deep tenebrous dark-
Crying into the night's breast

We watch the old cease to breathe-
Mourners in a manner of speaking
Uttering truths that lurk between
The boundaries of our skin
A conjoined pain-
The burden of humanity
That gnashes our bodies and
Tears dirges from our tired souls

We commune in broken laughter
Entirely, imperfectly perfect

HEAT

Difficult to discern where one body begins or ends
They blend, pigments mixed in the heat of thick breath
He aspires to worship the cream of her lonely curves
The webs of blue veins cracking
The breasts that reach upwards
Towards an unappeasable Heaven-
A drowning in the unspooled
Hair clenched in the night's teeth
A day that eclipses itself in a movement of color

He straddles her on dark stilts -
A spider wading through spilled milk
He immerses his hands inside her body-
Past the bones to pry a moan from her
And fasten it to his dark neck
He watches the room flower with petals
Of succulent flames as he slides
His tongue across her smooth arches
Welded together by elemental fusion
Their body screeches like a falcon - siring heat
Birthing diamonds

DISEMBODIED DREAM

Roiling bells bruise their iron bones
As the prostrated dreamer howls through the lot
A Gordian summer screaming to a sinking phone booth
As birds hide beneath newsprint and waves devour
It stinks, here- a wet death reek
That dampens the fibers of his coat
He trudges the nowhere of slumbering towers
Towards abysses of loose pilings and torments
Somewhere, a jaded mariner trades
Stories with an absentee father-
An engineer mourning the loss of his son-
A hemorrhaged sky beating the sun like a gong
The stranger wishes to say something to
These forlorn ghosts when he meets them-
However, the thought eludes him-
A dream rescuing its memory from a burning house

ONLY HE CAN SING

Plains hewed by water's axe
And wind's venomous sword
A face beneath one's feet
Gnawing fraught angles of stone
A gorgon's breath bathes the bloody pearls
A rancid laugh breaking a star's back
Night flakes from scampering water
A noose snapping the grass' neck
The watcher carries an empty chest
He thinks to repeat the words
That only he can hear-
He dreams of clouds in
Occult formations
Of days of lisping thunder
And Gordion snakes
The air tastes bitter, here-
Its mineral rust a fever in the blood
A time of sowing and passing
A moment of agonized laughter
A song that only he can sing

SYNTACTIC

Dream storm brilliant mercy
Itinerant of night of fulsome gold
When in dispatches the fault of verse
Paper tiger in the folded tome
Books upon books heaping

Lineages of roses my succulent scream
The bones of my joyous mouth
My determined echo howling of the voice
The screeching of the endless void

Mercy's brilliant dream
Time of throttled birds tonguing pages
Arrant argonauts pilfering the feast
Limelight serpent settling in the east

MADAM MAGPIE

Carve smoke with your
Immaculate breasts Madam Magpie
I kiss the waves of your porcelain arches
As you dangle from the bones of an ashen photo
Make me stir the milk of your body with my
Burnt hand and watch-
And settle like a moth on the lantern of my face
Brush me from your body and choke me
With garlands of pearls, as I whittle afternoons
Thieving sap from the marrow of your flawless ribs
Let my tongue carve your marbled shadow
As I hoard your moans like a miser
Slash my mouth with your immaculate breasts,
Madam Magpie - close me inside
The locket of your dreams
Bury me in the diffident dark
Of your beautiful laughter

JOYCE

I sail the clouds of your body
Marveling at the way your lips
Perch and hunger the sea

Your skin feeds me its elegant sentences
While you spill across the darkness of my body

Nefertiti poet I lacquer your patrician soles
With my willing mouth as Cairo scratches her neck
And mendicants sizzle within the shadows of mosques

You are ghostly now, Pharaoh's daughter

I watch orgasms bloom across
The shadowy monuments of your breasts-

An ibis god longing for your pantheon

Warm sand lingering where I carve a native tongue
Be one with me, my ruined sister

TIME

Joyful prayers hollow
The flightless bones
Over time, knuckles beat
Cheeks to meal
Grinding the predatory angles
Time waiting to drop the cudgel

Dull hammering of days
Against the scorched anvil
Night tasting on rust and minerals
Blood teasing the throat
I am quickened and alive
As morning unlocks its blade
And wakes me with keen slashes

Time never waits for time
Nor does it wash its hands
In the cold lake of my ribs
Nor does it care about the
Unpaid bills or my stomach
Time waits for nothing

AGAIN

I see Paris caress your
Face with thickening shadows
As I mouth the ache of
Your body - a prayer
That bleeds its way to Heaven
And leaves an ache in my bones
I dream of tasting the textile of your
Immaculate flesh
I'd roll you across the landscape of my tongue
To swallow the flames of your
Beautiful feathers- that part of you that tears
My heart from its cover and scatters its pages
My mouth longs to write its filth across you-
Or carve the grottoes of your center-
That soft line that longs for shade
Please, sharpen yourself and split me in half
Let me bury my hatchet in your arches
Or shriek across your profligate seasons
Kill me with the dagger of your little deaths
Again and again

SCORPION SONG

Someone once whispered that they
Watched you stir clouds with a stolen femur
As a pterodactyl interrogated you about Dadaism
And the lives of dead poets-
When the sun tidies its flooded room-
There is only the turtle and its
Temple of endless chambers
And a thrush roosting on a gloomy stone
Art breaks the gears of your enigmatic clock-
That leporine heart that sings its arias of color
To a theater filled with someone else's junk

You write postcards to the angry
Ghosts that sweep the streets clear of memory
You, a closet filled with someone else's clothing
Long to be eaten by clouds of moths
John, you are the emperor of flimflam
Of the most precious sort -
May you thrive in a flourish of blushing ink
In a brothel of stolen pigment
May you beat the day clean of its boredom
May you dip your fingers in the milk of empty pages

THE EYE

A sea of clouds swims in the eye
A clot of blood in the horizon's iris

The sea calls to itself and fills
Its chapeau with salt

Subverted, the eye becomes
A glorious doorway-

An almond balanced on
A tongue

The body draped like damp
Laundry across a chair

The scraped fruit glistening
Within sacred angles

The mariposa of a sigh
Kissing the mirror

LISBOA

O this fractured conversion
The wounded lyre playing
The narrow streets
Ode to the young girl threading
Hands with invisible bodies
The dark curves of her sweat
Tasting the heat of soft diamonds
Diaphanous dreams sleeping
Within a hawk's shadow
Shark swimming upward

Call to prayer in the urine
Of a saber bloodying the morning
Confections of mourners
Scurrying beneath the newsstand
Beaches of scorched sand
English by way of accent
Agonizing faces hidden in shadow

SONNET OF WIND AND SUN

Octavio, hack me with the blade
Of your volcanic hand-
With the terse stone of the mountains
Nourished by ice
I listen to your teeth
Cling to the stomachs of ancient ruins
To the secret places better left hidden
To a wound that refuses to heal
Octavio, breathing octaves of
Furtive elk to crown solemn hills

I cannot bear the pain flowering
In the crystalline pools of my hand
I see you standing, ancient tree
Half your face wreathed in flame

ECLIPSE

Queen of a thousand swords
Plant your feet in the soil
Of my aching sleep
Flower in the cup of
My empty hands
Nourish me
Nourish me
Sweet body of the silk shawl
Painful harmony of the white arms
Cut my glass with your breasts
Stir my blood in the cauldron
Of your hips
Lay with me in the flames
Of this doomed village
Lie to me in the death of
Of this cursed season
I wish us to end this filthy
Chapter while we lick our hurts
While the sun sweeps dust from
Its porch and furtive beasts hide
Drape across my broken hip
Tease my lips with your small finger
Shelter me, my poisoned eclipse!

BREAKING

As we lick this chapter clean
Of the syntax of our bodies
I nourish the flood that
Drags its fingers through this lonely city

The eye remains a desolate
Window in your heart
The door that refuses to close
Your voice - the ache of its sound

Old ghosts barter for time as
We sing the stars to guide us
The days shutter their stores and
Set Fire to their wares
All the while our skin sings

Our Bones scream verse that no one
Longs to hear - songs of love
And acidic hate - a scorpion's sting of longing
Fire in a river of blood

You, my beloved cauldron, are released
Gather your wounded birds
Your thorns and your pride
Play me the contumely of your laugh
Leave the light on; close the door behind you

RECOUNT

The shriek of the city buttons
Its winter coat as clouds
Argue with the sky
And empty their trash along
The boulevard of drunk saints
And traffic vendors

Call me Mr. Smoke
Or the prophet of Mephistopheles
That errant margin of error
That loiters on the sinister bank
And hoards his verse like a miser
Call me Manuel Angel

Call me nothing but Father Timepiece
The prince of broken clocks
And stolen watches
Call me the fool of the breast-shaped hills
The dove who abandons its shadow
The pie that remains uneaten

DROWN

Swim with the scales of your hands
Your mermaid sibilants braving the
Fathoms of a drowning clock
Bury the art of your sleep in
This desert of pigments
This waste of bone and leaning crosses
Write me the ache of a sonnet
And kiss me with the doorway of your mouth
See me through the agony of these phases
These months of incompetence that
Encumber me like a millstone
Sing to me, Rusalka, as I drown in myself
As I reach for you as though you were a wet branch
Free me from the prison of my body
Save me from saving myself

FINAL SONNET

He listens to the resonant bell
For lingering melodies-
Verdigris clinging to copper and brass
He hears himself in the architecture
Of sublime chaos-
Crowing of iridescent sticks
And reversed blessings
Outside, sidewinders burn curves
In feminine hills
A blush of moonlight abstracts

In splotches of green shadows
Somewhere, an aged body
Screams to hold its heart
Within its ribs

PHOTO

The angular neck
Joy of sacred geometry
The butterfly of lips
Beaded with pearls of sweat
Her body unspooled in
Gleams of warm amethyst
And hair snagged in the sky's teeth
Joy raises its kite
To crucify a voluptuous shadow
While light kisses the space between
The tanned breasts-
A sigh overturning a lit candle

ESTRELLA DE NOCHE

Plant yourself in me
Estrella de Noche

Bury me in the womb of your heart
Estrella de Noche

Part your hair like water
Estrella de Noche

Feed me the olives of your breasts
Estrella de Noche

Let my teeth drown in your skin
Estrella de Noche

LORCA'S SONNET

Lorca hands me his heart
While I pour orchids in a chalice
And shake hands with the morning
Breaking the wheel of a chariot
And piecing myself together
He speaks to me from the depths
Of the ocean's ink
From the moon that's broken in
His night's hair
And the death head's predatory roost

I watch thorns sprout from his mouth
As the scorpion of his tongue
Stings my ears-
His words sewing black tears in my heart

CHEMISE

Blue as the petals of a bruise
The artist inhabits the voice of
His thirsty hands
Beautiful ghost, the day
Cups your etiolated breast
As you stare westward

Your muslin skin sick for light
Sick of the darkness that threads
Between fingers
Your eyes close as thick
Fingers stir the murmuring sea
Of your hair

Stained fingers unfold your flower
To summon bitten lips and gentle sighs
The chemise slides from thin shoulders
And reveals the ennui of your sharp chest
He gathers you like a pile of elegant bones
You give yourself to him - a broad, pristine canvas

CREATION SONG

Let my hands map the seas of your breasts
While my mouth becomes the beak
That tears the sky from its yolk

I watch a sea of maddening stars
Devour the night's flesh
As a scream reverberates across your ribs
And I whet the blade of my body

Carve through me, my immaculate dove
Singe me with the heat of yes

Pulverize me with the ancient monument
Of your dance
The Jade heaviness of your sweat
To shatter my hips

Chisel your name across the remains of
My face as the moon flips its coin
And planets ovulate

Watch me die a slow, feathery death
As the day strangles its shadow
And an ox of dead seasons snaps its tether

Be with me here and now in this
Doomed haven of bodies

I am clay awaiting the coarse
Wedge of your hands

That which both sculpts and is sculpted

Matthew Bottiglieri began writing poems during his adolescence. His appreciation and understanding of poetics developed while studying with Susan Howe, Irving Feldman, Robert Creeley, and Charles Bernstein, at the University at Buffalo.

Matthew currently resides with his wife, Jennifer Lees, in Portland, Oregon. In addition to poetry, Matthew enjoys jiu-jitsu, long walks, and strong coffee.

If you have enjoyed this work, please be sure to follow Matthew Bottiglieri via Instagram at:
@hector_verse

www.ingramcontent.com/pod-product-compliance
Lightning Source LLC
LaVergne TN
LVHW041300080426
835510LV00009B/818